THE 5 STEPS TO CHANGING YOUR LIFE

JOHN A. ANDREWS

Copyright © 2007 by John A. Andrews
ISBN 978-0-983-1419-3-8
Cover Art: Job "Jobie" Bakama
Cover Photo: Tracy Olson
Photo: Adrian Carr

i

THE 5 STEPS TO CHANGING YOUR LIFE

The sources of our drinking water are always heavily guarded and protected from intrusion and contaminants. People protect their bodies from the weather and other elements. And yet, few take the time to protect their thought source — the mind.

Imagine your best friend comes over to visit one day, and in his hands are two heavy bags. You offer him a seat, and then sit on your recliner and adjust it to a comfortable position. "What's in the bags?" you ask. He immediately opens one of them and deposits its contents, full of grime and filth, onto your nice clean carpet. As your nostrils react to the stench, he opens the other bag. Do you encourage him to dump more contaminants into your habitat? Of course not!

So, consider this example in terms of your mind. How do you treat the situation if a friend dumps garbage into your thought source? Do you say, "Thank you very much for the pollutants; could you please deposit some more?" or do you put the breaks on his toxin distribution extravaganza?

- John A. Andrews

TABLE OF CONTENTS

CHAPTER:

This book is dedicated to my mother, Elaine Louisa Andrews, who lived a life of dedication and service to her church and community, and to my three sons: Jonathan, Jefferri and Jamison, who keep me filled with passion and purpose.

INTRODUCTION

Martin Luther King Jr., one of the greatest dreamers who ever lived, declared: "Take the first step in faith. You don't have to see the whole staircase. Just take the first step."[1]

I'm in my forties, and as you might imagine, scores of individuals have stepped into my life: some for a reason, some for a season and others for a lifetime. Some have talked the talk, some have walked the walk, and others have done both.

Each brought with them a reflection of the experiences — both good and bad — they've had along life's way. They weren't born the person they grew to become. Rather, day-by-day and year-by-year, they acquired their personal definition from the books they read and the people with whom they associated.

There's truth to this maxim: "Show me your friends and I'll tell you who you are." If you hang out with bank robbers you could end up driving the getaway car, and if you associate with pigs, you'll soon be rolling in the mud. Kids who wind up in gangs join them primarily to fulfill a need for community, and soon, they prey on society to support that community and attain identity within the group. Through con-version to Christianity, though, a gang-banger can dust himself off to lead a church or become a mentor to struggling youth.

Paul, once a persecutor of Christians, encountered a changed life on the road to Damascus when struck by a bright light from heaven. Following three days of blindness, he regained his sight by the hand of a disciple named Ananias, and immediately turned his life around, preaching Jesus as the Son of God (Acts 9:1-20).

So, yes, you can change your life and, yes, you can become the person you desire to become. Is it going to be easy? Probably not; effective change is not a Jack and the Beanstalk scenario. It's more like a seasonal transition. During autumn, leaves die and fall to the ground before winter steps in, and like the seasons, change is a process. Real change doesn't happen over night.

Becoming who you want to become is going to take work, as does raising a child, building a successful marriage, getting a degree or mastering a craft. Is it possible? It has been done. Can you do it? Only if you think you can. Will you lift yourself up by your own boot straps? Leaders aren't born; they are made. Is change worth the effort? Real change starts on the inside. "You cannot travel within and stand still without."[2] Your greatest achievement was at first, and for some time, just a thought.

One thing is for sure: If you grasp and apply these five steps that I'm about to give you, not only will you climb to insurmountable heights in your life and career, but you'll also have more joy, more friends, more love, more money, more passion and a deep sense of spiritual and intellectual satisfaction.

As your guide, it's imperative that I prepare you with simple guidelines. Upon receiving the idea to write this book, inspirational thoughts flooded my mind, allowing me to complete its first draft in one week. To get the most out of it, you need passion, blended with a burning desire to change your life.

If you're ready to take on the world, you should read this book in its entirety before you go to bed. Do not create a dam; as a stream of water desires to reach the ocean, so train yourself to do likewise. Once you've finished reading, re-read the five steps as a refresher course. I'll see you at the summit of life's staircase.

The oak sleeps in the acorn; the bird waits in its egg; and in the highest vision of the soul a waking angel stirs.

— James Allen

1
CHANGE YOUR THOUGHTS

According to the great philosopher James Allen, "Man is made or unmade by himself; in the armory of thought he forges the weapons by which he destroys himself; he also fashions the tools by which he builds for himself heavenly mansions of joy and strength and peace."[1]

What is thought? Thought is a mental action that influences the world around us. Much like we see electricity at work, we see manifestations of thought everywhere. It functions as a sort of wireless electri-city.

Thought is revealed in the actions of children, adults and animals. It acts as a terrific force with unlimited power.

If you are reading this book in a room or anywhere outdoors within a stone's throw from civilization, take a look around. You'll realize that you're looking at objects — including the book in your hands — created from someone's thoughts. All that you see on the outside first came from within. Thought is the one thing over which you have absolute control; only you can decide what you do with your thought.

Your way of thinking starts with individual thoughts, whether good, bad or ugly. Your subconscious prod-uces thought, and your five senses give birth to thought based on your present environment. God and the devil are the two other sources of thought.

The five senses deal with the mind, but God deals with the heart and speaks to us through the Holy Spirit. After Jesus' ascension into heaven, his disciples received the outpouring of the Holy Spirit from God and thus performed miraculous deeds. "God says: 'In the last days I will pour out of my Spirit on all kinds of people. Your sons and daughters will prophesy. Your young men will see visions, and your old men will dream dreams.'" (Acts 2:17) In most cases, the mind has to be ready to utilize thoughts from God, just like the ground has to be prepared before seeds are sown therein.

Thoughts enter your mind whether you want them to or not. They arrive every waking and sleeping moment of your life, as both initial data and original ideas, and sometimes turn into action. In his book *Hung by the Tongue*, author Francis P. Martin explains, "An imagination is intent to do something about what you've been thinking; a stronghold is when the choice is not yours anymore, but you have submitted your will to the thought."[2] Imaginations are images, and strongholds are responsible for turning thoughts into reality. Once a thought arrives, the imagination goes to work on it, and if a monopoly is placed on it, that thought becomes reality.

Let's say, for instance, that the thought of stealing comes to mind. It's up to you to dismiss or keep that thought. If you choose to entertain the thought, it will become an imagination, or intent to steal. If that thought is caressed, it will evolve into a stronghold and you will end up stealing, unless you submit the temptation to the power of God and, with His help, avoid yielding to it.

You must decide what you're going to do with a thought. Will you discard it, throwing it into your recycle bin, or will you employ it? The thoughts you utilize will shape your destiny — either a life of mediocrity or a life of greatness. Evidence of the latter is seen in the lives of Columbus, Copernicus, Gandhi, Winston Churchill, Mother Teresa, Abraham Lincoln, Martin Luther King Jr., Helen Keller and many others, who, out of their thoughts, accomplished great things. Imagine what would have happened to our civili-zation if they had discarded those thoughts.

DISCARDED THOUGHTS

"Both poverty and riches are the offspring of thought," author Napoleon Hill says in his book *Think and Grow Rich*.[3]
If you're not careful, abandoned thoughts can come back to haunt you. Have you ever given up a thought or idea that came to you, only to later see it achieved by someone else? People frequently tell me they have a great idea for a screenplay. My usual response is, "Why don't you write it or have someone else write it for you?" But nine times out of 10, they fall asleep on the idea, only to later watch it unfold on the movie screen.

On the other hand, you're constantly bombarded by negative thoughts that, if entertained, will have an adverse effect on the way you do life. Those thoughts — ones that belittle, dehumanize and keep you in bondage — are the ones you must change. You must let go of thoughts that tell you that you came from nothing, will never amount to anything and are no good. "What makes you think you have it in you to accomplish anything worthwhile?" those thoughts say. "You failed yesterday and you are destined to fail again today." The truth is, nobody has ever accompli-shed anything worthwhile without changing those kinds of thoughts.

LESSONS FROM MOM

When I was a little boy growing up on the islands of Saint Vincent and the Grenadines, my mom would say, very philosophically: "What you give out in your right hand you're going to receive in your left. You can do whatever you set in your heart and mind to accomplish. If you can think it, you can do it." For a while, I thought she was too immersed in the Word. But some of it did resonate in my delicate mind.

TURNING THOUGHTS INTO REALITY

I was obsessed with becoming a police officer when I grew up, for example, so I studied policemen and prayed to God that someday I would become one. Today, the profession doesn't intrigue me in the same way it used to, but most of the screenplays I've written are about police officers or have something to do with law enforcement. What my mother told me as a child, I've realized, has merit. Thoughts hold magic and power.

As a dad, I make it a habit to tell my three sons, ages 11, 9 and 8, not only that I love them and am proud of them, but also that they can do anything they can imagine. They believe in their ability and, as a result, the two eldest have already embarked upon the task of collaboratively writing their first Disney-type screenplay. They are developing the will to win.

BELIEVE IT, CONCEIVE IT

In *Think and Grow Rich*, Hill talks about a secret hidden in the pages. If you're ready to receive it, he says, you already possess one half; you'll acquire the other half once it reaches into your mind. This secret, he adds, cannot be had at any price by those who are not intentionally searching for it. So, I read the book in hot pursuit and with an open mind, believing in order to conceive. Ideas came to me in abundance and I juggled them. My favorites? "Your own thoughts and desires serve as the magnet which attracts units of life, from the great ocean of life out there." And, "All achievement, all earned riches, have their begin-ning in an idea." [4]

Belief is a powerful force that drives thought. Good thoughts are usually born out of inspiration, and to be inspired, you must be in alignment with God. At one point during Jesus' ministry, His disciples failed to cast a demon out of a little boy; they lacked faith. But Jesus rebuked the demon and he departed from the child. "Later, the disciples came to Jesus asking, 'Why couldn't we cast him out?' And Jesus said unto them, 'Because of your unbelief: for verily I say unto you, "If you have faith as a mustard seed, you shall say unto this mountain, 'Remove hence to yonder place;' and it shall remove;" and nothing shall be impossible unto you'." (Matt. 17:19-20)

In the story of David and Goliath, David's peers probably

saw a mountain standing in his way but his faith in the Lord produced an unexpected outcome in battle. "When Goliath looked at David and saw that he was only a boy, tanned and handsome, he looked down on David with disgust. He said, 'Do you think I am a dog, that you come at me with a stick?' He used his gods' names to curse David; He said to David, 'Come here I'll feed your body to the birds of the air and the wild animals!' But David said unto him, 'You come to me using a sword and two spears. But I come to you in the name of the Lord All-Powerful, the God of the armies of Israel! You have spoken against him.'" (1 Sam. 17:42-45) David saw the giant as too big to miss and slew him with a few stones and a slingshot.

Belief inspires one to do the seemingly impossible. An inspired person is apt to break bonds of restraint in his or her mind in order to accomplish tasks in record-breaking style.

Through inspiration, Chicago Bulls player Michael Jordan pursued respect for himself and his team by scoring three times his jersey number as he dropped 69 points on the Cleveland Cavaliers in March, 1990. Whenever you have an inspired thought, you must trust it and act on it.

THE WILL TO SUCCEED

After the Screen Actors Guild commercial strike in 1998, compounded by the effects of 9/11, I struggled as a commercial actor. Previously I'd had a very successful streak of national television spots, landing nine within a 13-month stretch. So off I went search-ing for ways to make things happen. I wasn't going to allow the industry drought to stop me.

Out of the universe, a hunch nudged me: "Why not become a filmmaker? That's what most successful people in Hollywood do." Some of my acquaintances were already climbing that ladder of success, so I submitted to the idea.

At the time, I had no experience in filmmaking, except that which I had picked up on a few movie sets. Nonetheless, I was determined to succeed. There was a classic 1970's film I liked so much that I thought about remaking it. For the next three weeks, I made phone calls to find out who held the rights to my intended pet project. When I finally made contact with the studio, a woman answered the phone and told me they were not interested in selling the rights to a third party.

That statement didn't sit well with me. You see, my plane had already taken off, the fasten-your-seat-belt signs were already extinguished, and the hostess was serving the beverage of the day. I composed myself, contacted a writer friend whose script was recently optioned by a major studio, and asked him to assist me in writing my script. He did one of the best things a person can do for another: instead of giving me a fish, he showed me how to fish by sending me guide-lines for writing a screenplay. I got busy. My mantra echoed, "I'll write my own. I'll show them. They'll be begging for my work someday." My imaginary air-plane was swiftly gaining altitude.

The initial draft of that first screenplay was completed within 29 days. Later, I gladly showed one of my scripts to an acquaintance of mine who is a director. He not only told me I was such a novice, but also said it was the worst screenplay he had ever seen. That hit home like a ton of bricks, and after a few sleepless nights I went back to the drawing board. About a year later, he read one of my action thrillers and remarked,

"I think you have the knack, guy. Not too many people can do it this way."

Two of my original screenplays are currently in the pre-production phase, but that wouldn't have hap-pened if I hadn't followed through with my thoughts and kept going. If I hadn't coupled belief with thought, my ideas might have been left in the recycle bin.

THOUGHTS LEFT IN THE RECYCLE BIN

John F. Kennedy, the youngest and one of the greatest United States presidents, said this: "The problems of the world cannot possibly be solved by the skeptics or cynics whose horizons are limited by the obvious realities. We need men who can dream of things that never were."[5]

It should alarm you that the ideas that could beckon a revolution and solve most of the world's problems, including AIDS, cancer and Alzheimer's disease, may be sitting idle in the recycle bins of people's minds. People who allow their thoughts to sit idle are content with inside-the-box thinking, filled with what I call "the could-have-been syndrome." That's the way millions of people live their lives. They create a worldwide "I don't have what it takes" epidemic; as one of my associates says, they have no guts.

Every business, building, highway, school, house, song, screenplay, relationship — everything — begins with a thought. In the book *The Magic of Thinking Big*, David Schwartz writes, "Think: 'I can do better.' The best is not unattainable. There's room for doing everything better. Nothing in the world is being done as well as it could be. And when you think, 'I can do better,' ways to do better will appear."[6] Thinking that way will ignite your creative powers and, like the pent-up flow released from a dam, you will become relentless.

USED THOUGHTS

In his book *The Magic of Believing*, Claude Bristol states, "There never was a period in history when we should study our own thoughts more, try to under-stand them, and learn how to improve our position in life by drawing upon the great source of power that lies within each of us."[7]

How can you tell which thoughts are good and which thoughts are bad? Think of the mind — your storehouse of thoughts — as an empty hard drive in a computer. It knows nothing except what you put into it. The real you is your heart, or your spirit, from where all issues of life flow. I've made it a habit for over a decade to feed my computer - the mind with "good" by reading and listening to inspirational material just before bed. Sometimes I fall asleep while listening. But because my subconscious is still awake while I sleep, it absorbs most of the information. I've noticed that at times throughout the day, inspirational thoughts and messages hit me. And more often than not, when I'm in a situation where it's crucial to find the right words, I'm able to deliver.

Upon acting on the idea to write this book, I felt as if the floodgates of my heart and mind opened, pouring out a storehouse of inspiration. I was directed to previously read books in my library and even to the page, and the highlighted quote, needed for the appropriate insert.

When it comes to thought, only you can determine what is installed on your computer. Remember, input equals output. What you sow you shall also reap.

THINKING OUTSIDE OF THE BOX

Thought largely determines the "haves" from the "have nots" in today's society. Author Victor Hugo said, "Nothing else in the world ... not all the armies ... is so powerful as an idea whose time has come."[8] And Warren Bennis, in his book *On Becoming a Leader*, writes, "A leader is, by definition, an innovator. He does things other people haven't done or don't do. He does things in advance of other people. He makes new things. He makes old things new."[9]

I believe we all have the ability to change what we touch for the better, and if we take advantage of our God-given potential, we'll leave this world a better place than we found it. After all, we were formed by the One who created everything; without Him, nothing was made. He loves always and gives bountifully when we serve Him in spirit and in truth. If in His image we were formed and molded, why should we profess any form of inhibition? Why do we let small thinking control us? Could it be that we refrain from being plugged into the source — our infinite God? What happens to a river that refuses to draw water from its source?

If we think with a mindset of giving, we entertain abundance, and if we think with an attitude of withholding, we invite lack. The Bible states in Luke 6:38, "Give, and you will receive. You will be given much. Pressed down, shaken together, and running over, it will spill into your lap. The way you give to others is the way God will give to you." As the source gives to the stream so ought the stream to impart to the ocean.

In 1980, I was greeted by the Statue of Liberty, subway stations, taxis and massive pedestrian traffic upon my entrance into New York City. A few years before, still living in the Islands, I had seen pictures of the city's greatest landmarks through a viewfinder on loan from a friend. I dreamed of living in the Big Apple, and I finally made it. After years of balancing odd jobs, seeds for my acting career were planted and took root.

While I drove taxis there in New York, my yearning to become an actor gnawed at me. One evening I picked up a passenger in Queens on his way to Manhattan, and we struck up a conversation. He said he was an actor and thought I had a great presence and would look powerful on screen. I told him I had been thinking about the possibility of acting for quite some time. Before exiting the cab, he not only gave me the name of his acting school and a contact person, but also left his number in case I needed further assistance with my enrollment at Lee Stras-burg Institute. The rest is history.

Moving to Los Angeles has, in more ways than one, broadened my horizons, enhanced my thinking, and expanded my vision. My experiences gained from "The University of Hard Knocks" have given me the idea and the drive to write, and today, this book is a result of that seed-planting-fruit-bearing thought.

PROTECTING YOUR THOUGHT SOURCE

Claude Bristol states: in The Magic of Believing, "The secret of success lies not without, but within, the thoughts of man."[10]

The sources of our drinking water are always heavily guarded and protected from intrusion and contaminants. People protect their bodies from the weather and other elements. And yet, few take the time to protect their thought source — the mind.

Imagine your best friend comes over to visit one day, and in his hands are two heavy bags. You offer him a seat, and then sit on your recliner and adjust it to a comfortable position. "What's in the bags?" you ask. He immediately opens one of them and deposits its contents, full of grime and filth, onto your nice clean carpet. As your nostrils react to the stench, he opens the other bag. Do you encourage him to dump more contaminants into your habitat? Of course not.

So, consider this example in terms of your mind. How do you treat the situation if a friend dumps garbage into your thought source? Do you say, "Thank you very much for the pollutants; could you please deposit some more?" or do you put the breaks on his toxin distribution extravaganza?

THE POWER OF THOUGHT

Napoleon Hill states in his book *Think and Grow Rich*, "It has been said that man can create anything which he can imagine."[11] Pascal had this to say: "Man's greatness lies in his power of thought."[12] Thoughts are magnetic. They will attract people that support them and an environment in which they can grow, producing after their kind.

You, too, can attract what you want, and the strength of the thought vibration will determine the strength of its attraction. A mere wish lacks the tenacity neces-sary to get unleashed.

By changing your thoughts you will change your expressions, and eventually, your world. Everything you accomplish or fail to accomplish in life will be a direct result of the thoughts you cherish in your mind and the words that come out of your mouth. Wherever you are right now, everything you've experienced has prepared you for this moment in time.

Our achievements of today are but the sum total of our thoughts of yesterday. You are today where the thoughts of yesterday have brought you and will be tomorrow where the thoughts of today take you.[13] — Pascal

God spoke the world into existence . . .

2
CHANGE YOUR WORDS

The power of words and their influence over making things happen goes all the way back to the pre-Eden days. The world was empty without form and darkness covered the ocean. "Then God said, 'Let there be light,' and there was light." (Gen. 1:2-3) He spoke and it was done.

YOU GET WHAT YOU SAY

James 3:12 confirms: "My brothers and sisters, can a fig tree make olives, or can a grapevine make figs? No! And a well of salty water cannot give good water."

Most people tend to slack off when it comes to speaking the right words; some refuse to because of their unbelief, while others aren't educated when it comes to speaking what they want into existence. The farmer exercises faith by putting seed into the ground and expectantly waiting for a plant to emerge. Then he waters and fertilizes the soil, destroys the weeds, and prunes the plant in anticipation of a harvest. If he doesn't, starvation may be imminent. He sows with time and effort, and he reaps what he sows. Words out of your mouth are like seeds sown into the universe. If they're good seeds, they have the poten-tial to bring forth good fruit, and vice versa.

Your words affect your destiny, and what you allow yourself to think and express characterizes who you are. Some people, even so-called Christians, believe that they were born to be poor. Others believe they must settle for a life of mediocrity. Some misquote 1 Timothy 6:10, "The love of money causes all kinds of evil," by saying that money itself is the root of all evil. They abhor that evil and express doubt habitually in other areas of life. No wonder 80 percent of the world's wealth and other good things are hoarded by 20 percent of the population.[1]

Proverbs 12:25 reads, "Worry is a heavy load, but a kind word cheers you up." It's a given that a farmer can't sow apple seeds and anticipate a harvest of oranges. Delivering good news to someone will not only lift their spirits, but also yours in return. If the right words aren't spoken, limits are placed on what you can and will accomplish in your lifetime; you possess what you confess.

When my ex-wife and I got married, her objective was to have three sons. She not only let me know her desire but also gladly told everyone with whom she came in contact. Our first seven years of marriage were kid-free, but within the next five years we were blessed with Jonathan, Jefferri and Jamison. She devoured *Hung by the Tongue*, and coupled with unwavering faith, got what she said.

In the book, author Francis Martin writes, "If you criticize people, you'll reap criticism. If you judge people, you will be judged. If you bless people you will receive blessings in return."[2] What you say you will certainly get.

MB, a young man in his mid-20's, moved from Northern California to Hollywood over a year ago in pursuit of the Hollywood dream. I met him at our church while he was still getting acclimated and we created a bond; he has admirable leadership potential. As most people who move to the entertainment industry capital know, you take the job you can get until you get the job you want. So, he took a management position at a retail store, a job which demanded him showing up to work on Sundays. I could tell he was burnt out Sunday after Sunday.

A few months ago, MB told me that he had had enough and was ready to move on. I saw him a week ago and he mentioned that he would be interviewing with one of the top talent agencies in the industry. He was confident about landing the job. He said, "I'm going to get it." I was a little hesitant but suggested an alternative agency just in case. He looked me dead in the eye and said "John, I'm going to get it." A few days ago my phone rang. It was MB and he had gotten the job. MB spoke what he wanted and got it.

WHAT YOU SAY TO YOUR KIDS

The Bible says, "Train children to live the right way, and when they are old, they will not stray from it." (Prov. 22:6) This applies to the words sown in a child's delicate, fertile mind. At an early age, seeds are planted in a kid's mind by a parent, babysitter, guardian or environment. If those happen to be weed seeds, that child will likely grow up with a very poor self-image. Later on in life, if he desires healthy self-esteem, he may turn to therapy, guidance or associ-ation to pluck those deep-rooted poisonous plants. Even if this process destroys the weeds, some of their roots still remain. As the farmer knows, no matter what he does, some weeds spring up again and again. That's why most people have to keep diluting the "toxin" in their minds by constantly putting in the good stuff — speaking the right words. If left untreated, symptoms result in "toxic people," and the world is full of them. That's why it ticks me off when I hear parents tell their kids the following:

- You'll never amount to anything.

- You're a disgrace.

- You're a lazy good-for-nothing.

- Keep doing what you're doing and you'll spend the rest of your life in prison.

- You're a bum.

- I don't want to have anything to do with you.

- I'm not your father/mother.

- You belong in the mental asylum.

- You're such a slob.

- Your brother is better than you.

On and on the list goes. Most kids today suffer from low self-esteem that they didn't create. Kendall White, writing on Youth Motivation states: "Many of today's youth suffer from negative attitudes and negative environments. Too many of our young people are being raised in environments, which subject them to numerous forms of abuse."[3] No wonder there are so many unwanted childhood pregnancies and hosts of juvenile detention centers.

Why can't parents tell their children that they're the best — that they love them and are proud of them? Parents usually cherish those sentiments during the embryonic stage, and then at birth and before they begin analyzing the person who has come into their lives. But somewhere along the way, those emotions fade.

Parents need to admit that they're not perfect — that they're a work in progress, too. And kids need to keep on hearing words of affirmation in order to possess a healthy self-image.

WHAT YOU SAY TO YOUR SPOUSE

Spouses sometimes have a similar problem support-ing and building up one another. Instead of voicing love and affirmation, they use phrases such as these:

- You're a born loser.

- You're the worst.

- You never do things right.

- I don't know why I married you.

- We've got the worst marriage.

- Everything is wrong with our relationship.

- Your friend is a better husband to his wife.

- You never do the dishes.

- We don't have enough money.

- Our life's a mess.

- You're always late.

- I want a divorce.

No wonder 50% of all first time marriages end in divorce within an average time of eleven years.[4] Most of them collapsing within the first five years. This might not be the case if couples would continue with the great words they uttered during courtship:

- You're the spice of my life.

- There's no me without you.

- It's amazing to watch you grow.

- You make me happy.

- We're a team.

- I love you and I'm proud of you.

- I was wrong; I'm sorry; I apologize.

What an effect this kind of speech could have on our divorce stats!

Words have the same effect on a person's life as gravity on objects in space. If you were to jump freely off the roof of a tall building, you would fall to the ground; there isn't an alternative. Words, too, can cause a person to fall, if thought gives way to a reckless decision. But if your mind, the storehouse of your thoughts, is controlled, it becomes easier to control the mouth. And you don't risk facing the inevitable danger of carelessly uttered words. Pro-verbs 13:2-3 says this: "People will be rewarded for what they say, but those who can't be trusted want only violence. Those who are careful about what they say protect their lives, but whoever speaks without thinking will be ruined."

WHAT YOU SAY TO YOURSELF

"The words you have said will be used to judge you." (Matt. 12:37) So many times I run into so-called Christians who give our Creator and their life a bad rap by the words they speak:

- I've got so much bad luck.

- I'm sick as a dog.

- I've got no money.

- Nobody loves me.

- I don't have what it takes to succeed.

- I can't stand them. They've got it better than me.

- I've prayed for it and it's just not working out.

They forget their tongue is a weapon with the ability to destroy them, the issuer, and the recipient. To guard against someone's reckless speech on your behalf, it's imperative that you speak your own words of faith. Words of faith attract God's blessing in much the same way as a magnet draws steel.

"When we put bits into the mouths of horses to make them obey us, we can control their whole bodies. Also a ship is very big, and it is pushed by strong winds. But a very small rudder controls a big ship, making it go wherever the pilot wants. It is the same with the tongue. It is a small part of the body, but it brags about great things. A big forest fire can be started with a little flame. And the tongue is like a fire. It is a whole world of evil among the parts of our bodies. The tongue spreads its evil through the whole body. The tongue is set on fire by hell, and it starts a fire that influences all of life. ... We use our tongues to praise our Lord and Father, but then we curse people, whom God made like himself. My brothers and sisters, this should not happen. Do good and bad water flow from the same spring?" (James 3:2-6, 9-11)

Proverbs 18:21 states, "What you say can mean life or death. Those who speak with care will be rewarded." Words, by the power of the Almighty God, created the universe and the body that you now live in. Your words mixed with faith will propel you toward your destiny.

CHANGING WHAT YOU SAY

Why are words so powerful? Because they govern our hearts and control our physical body, steering us toward our desired goals and dreams.

A few years ago, my senior pastor's wife was diagnosed with breast cancer. Though our church believes in miracles and the power of prayer, we watched her fight this disease with the power of words. I saw her a few times during her travail and found out that she carried around index cards with words of confession and affirmation; she didn't want anything to do with the sometimes fatal disease. Prayers were poured out on her behalf, and it's believed that she totally confessed her own healing. Today, she travels all over the world teaching people the power of the Word over sickness in the body. You cannot speak both sickness and disease and expect to
walk in good health.

What would your life be like if you were to use these motivating faith-filled words?

- No weapon formed against me shall prosper.

- "I can do all things through Christ which strengtheneth me." (Phil. 4:13 KJV)

- "The steps of a good man are ordered by the Lord." (Ps. 37:23 KJV)

- I refuse to renounce my self image, no matter what happens to me.

To paraphrase my favorite inspirational one-liners from Bishop T.D. Jakes messages:

- The battle is not mine; it belongs to the Lord.

- What God has for me no devil in hell can take.

- I was born to do this.

- The time has come for my change.
- God is taking me where no man has gone before.

- I must prosper.

- I can have what God says I can have.

- I will arise! I will finish.

- When it's all said and done, I'll come out of it.

- I'm the head and not the tail.

- You may whip some but not me. I'm going to force you to give up.

- I have what it takes for my dream.

- I'm a giant killer.

- I'm chosen. I can take less and do more with it.

- God wants me to be so blessed that I live in the land of much.
- God is opening doors for me that no man can shut.[5]

What a difference it will make in your Christian walk if, as the flood storms of life come against you, you remain immovable.

You ought to not just speak your desires but must also believe that what you say will come to pass. If you cultivate bad thoughts, the words you speak will, like the fruit of a poisoned vine, destroy you. As thought seeds grow through your spoken words, so will the change within you.

No longer will you step aside to let crusaders go by. Others will step aside for you because you are now a crusader.

— William Danforth

3
CHANGE YOUR ACTIONS

You possess a great and powerful asset that, if util-ized, will lift you to insurmountable heights in your life. The things that others call impossible will be yours for the taking. This asset I mention will not only bring you confidence, but will also give you total satisfaction and peace of mind.

You possess the power to change. Once you recognize that power and learn how to use it, changes in the way you act will be automatic. You'll become like a butterfly that has left its cocoon; your thoughts and words will have transformed you and you will be ready to take action. You will have purpose and dir-ection in your life. You will have said goodbye to indecision and welcomed success and prosperity into your life, blessing the lives of others in the process.

Your decisions influence how you will live the remainder of your life. Choice precedes action as day precedes night. Life moves swiftly, and you need to act before you're acted upon.

What actions are you willing to take in order to impact your life in a positive way? How strong is your courage? Do you want what you touch to turn to gold? Is there a thought seed you've sown with words of faith that you're now ready to prune and watch bear fruit? Are you ready to take some action?

This chapter, by far, is the most important in this book, and it's going to take some effort on your part. It's going to take giving up a humdrum life of leth-argy for one of bravery and fun.

Most people are content to sit back and wait for things to come to them. They're going through life waiting for their ships to come in when they've never even set sail. You may have all the talent in the world, but if you're hiding your light under a bushel, the world won't know it. You will only attract the world by going to it with your shining light. The world has to know that you exist.

TOMORROW PEOPLE

"Tomorrow People" are those who prefer to wait for their world to come to them instead of meeting it head on. They will tell you, in no uncertain terms, that they are going to get started tomorrow. The problem is, that tomorrow turns into another tomor-row, and then another tomorrow and another, and so on. Talent does not guarantee success. It's what you do with the talent that counts. When you move toward your world, your world moves toward you.

What limitations are you placing on yourself? Wouldn't you rather try to succeed and fail than do nothing at all? Are you waiting for tomorrow?

Some people like to watch things happen, some people like to wait for things to happen, some people like to wonder what will happen, and some people don't care what happens. But the action-driven person delights in making things happen. Keith DeGreen states in *Creating a Success Environment*, "Yesterday is a cancelled check; tomorrow is a promissory note."[1] If it's going to happen, it's up to you to strike that spark. Some people create, while others compete. Creating is where the rubber meets the road. A dream worth having is one worth fighting for because freedom is not free; it carries a massive price tag.

When I was a kid, my mom told me a story about a woman who would take her laundry to the river every day, sit down on a huge stone with the soap and laundry next to her, and pray to God that he'd send her help to wash the daily-increasing load. But help never came. She might have had faith, but she wasn't willing to do the work, and help never came. What are you willing to do with the gifts and abilities that have been given to you? Is your dare strong enough to cause you to swim upstream when others around you are content to float downstream? "Every fish that swims upstream is worth ten that loaf in lazy bays,"[2] William Danforth says in his book *I Dare You.*

I've seen so many people who just sit on their talent. They have no zest, vim, vitality, passion or sense of purpose. Nothing drives them. They are like a train without a caboose. And they wonder why others are moving ahead in life while they're not. They're waiting for someone to inject them with a dose of success or, like the woman with the laundry, praying that God will bless their idle deeds.

BECOME A CRUSADER

In his book, Danforth also writes this challenge: "I am looking for you, one of the audacious few, who will face life courageously, ready to strike at the heart of anything that is keeping you from your best; you intrepid ones behind whom the world moves for-ward."[3]

Additionally, he tells a story about a young man who was working as a second hand on a railroad. The man's thoroughness had won him an opportunity to work for a few days in a shipping office. During the interim, the superintendent asked this young substi-tute clerk for some vital facts and figures. The young man didn't know anything about bookkeeping, but he worked three days and three nights without sleep and had the facts ready for the superintendent when he returned. That act of decision and commitment later propelled him into the vice-presidency seat of his own company.[4]

A few years ago, I worked as a property manager for a residential complex. One of my tenants was a young producer who had just gone through a disheartening divorce. My three young boys and I had the chance to spend some time with him and his 3-year-old son, and I realized during our visits that he spent most of his time reading movie scripts. An associate of mine told me that one day, he saw him on an airplane with at least six scripts in his briefcase. Today, he's not only engaged to a great woman, but he's also one of the most successful independent film producers in Hollywood and owns a movie franchise that has grossed over $100 million a year for the past three years. He's what I call a true crusader.

Once you acquire the action habit, others have no choice but to step aside for you; you're a crusader, and the world always seems to make way for the person who knows where he's going. Even traffic on crowded streets makes way for a fire engine on a mission. Take one step forward and your enemies will run for cover.

CHART YOUR COURSE

Action cures fear. Become known for doing things. When you see something that you believe ought to be done, step up to the plate and hit the home run. Don't wait for conditions to be perfect. They never will. The losers in life always wait for an invitation to succeed. You have the right to be uncommon as you set and reach for your goals — and a life of which you can be proud. Former President Theodore Roosevelt stated: *"I choose not to be a common man. Me, it's my right to be uncommon if I can. I'll seek opportunity, not security. I do not wish to be a kept citizen — humbled and dulled by having the state look after me. I want to take the calculated risk, to dream and to build, to fail and to succeed. I'll refuse to live from hand to mouth. I'll prefer the challenges of life to the guaranteed existence. The thrill of fulfillment to the stale calm of Utopia. I will never cower before any master or bend to any friend. It is my heritage to stand erect, proud and unafraid, to think and act for myself and face the world boldly and say, "This I have done."* [5]

THE NEGATIVE OPINIONS OF OTHERS

What would my friends say? What would they think of me? How would my parents feel? Those are some of the concerns faced by someone who has decided to venture out on a new frontier.

When I decided to attend acting school back in New York, those closest to me thought I had fallen off the deep end. They dangled a rope for me by reminding me of how great I was at other things. Then, when the decision came to move to Los Angeles, they warned me that California is in danger of falling into the Pacific Ocean.

I refused to let small thinking chart my course in life. David Schwartz states in *The Magic of Thinking Big,* "Nothing — absolutely nothing — in this world gives you more satisfaction than knowing you're on the road to success and achievement. And nothing stands as a bigger challenge than making the most of your-self."[6] And Danforth exhorts in *I Dare You,* "I dare you to achieve something that will make the world point to you with even more pride than the present is pointing to those who have gone before you."[7]

How do you want to be counted? Danforth further challenges: "Are you content to have posterity look at your life so far and say, 'That is all he was capable of?' Or are you one of the priceless few, one of those with a restless feeling that someday you are going to climb to your rightful place of leadership? That someday you are going to create something worthy of your best?"[8]

As you change your thoughts, you will change your words, your actions, your character and, eventually, your world.

The only thing that walks back from the tomb with the mourners and refuses to be buried is the character of a man.

— J. R. Miller

4

CHANGE YOUR CHARACTER

"Man know thyself," the famous axiom urges. Who are you really, when no one is looking? Changing your character is the most thought-provoking, and sometimes dreaded, step toward changing your world. If you embrace this change, you are ready to swim upstream where, like a diamond in the rough, you'll become polished and will no longer remain hidden with your light under a bushel. Changing your character calls for that mustard-seed-like faith and self discipline that will enable you to scale moun-tains along the way.

YOUR CHARACTER DEFINES YOU

In August 1963 in a speech to civil rights supporters at the March on Washington, Martin Luther King Jr. declared, "I have a dream that my four little children will one day live in a nation where they will not be judged by the color of their skin but by the content of their character."[1] He wanted his family to be defined by their character.

When I was a little boy, my mom dragged my eight siblings and me to church every week, even if our worship attire had to be recycled. She insisted on our involvement. She was proud of us and the foundation that was being laid in the lives of her kids. That weekly two-mile walk each way not only wore out our shoes but also helped develop fortitude in us.

Immediately after my divorce in 2000, I found myself homeless. As a result of 9/11, TV commercial audi-tions were few and far between, and most of my cur-rently running commercial spots got cut. I watched as my savings accounts plummeted to zero.

My search for employment continued after my unemployment benefits expired, but it seemed like the spots of the leper were tattooed onto my body; no one opted to hire me. So I prayed. And fasting was automatic and habitual. But most importantly, my trials summoned the lessons in faith I had learned as a child. That faith merged with what I was learning, and my search for wisdom skyrocketed. My writing skills improved, too, so I continued writing.

I became a better listener during this time, and experienced the Holy Spirit speaking to me often in a still small voice, reminding me that I was chosen. I grew to believe that the world needed me as well as I needed it. My car became not only a place of rest but also an office after Starbucks closed its doors for the night. I wrote every day no matter what, focused on getting back on the horse. My mantra was like a broken record: you kick me when I'm down, but watch out when I get back up.

In retrospect, I realize that a tremendous groundwork was laid during my childhood, and I thank and applaud my parents (my mom as well as my dad, who died when I was 9) for what they did. My life has been one of testing, and through the fire I've emer-ged, stronger than when I went in and appreciative of the refining process.

Will you have to face the challenges I've faced? I hope not. But whatever challenges you might be going through right now, whether financial, health-related, or based on relationships or your career, you can come out of them if you realize that you are chosen and have unquenchable passion and purpose for your life. As Norman Vincent Peale said, "You can if you think you can."[2]

DEVELOPING PASSION AND PURPOSE

"But they that wait upon the Lord shall renew their strength; they shall mount up with wings as eagles; they shall run and not be weary; and they shall walk, and not faint." (Isa. 40:31 KJV)

I knew during my homelessness, as I counted pennies to afford food and a hotel room on the weekends for my three sons and me, that someday I would be called to contribute to society. And when that hap-pened, my readiness would be paramount. Deep down in every fiber of my being, I believed that and wanted to be able to stand when the dust settled. Since then, I've noticed that my life is constantly fueled with tremendous passion and purpose; I've left the cocoon behind along with the habits that kept me bound.

What do you want said of you when your physical journey has ended? Wouldn't you rather wear out than rust out? Is it your intent to achieve something that will make the future point to you with even more pride than the present is pointing to those who have gone before you? What is your purpose? Is it for a cause greater than yourself?

So many people resist change for fear of the unknown. But if they were to stretch outside of their comfort zone, they would be amazed at the beautiful rainbow waiting to pour down showers of blessing upon them. Most people don't want to stretch, and they go to their graves with music still inside of them.

Their epitaphs read: "No guts no glory."

If you've gotten this far and are committed to this journey, you have what it takes to finish strong. Life is about to obey *you*. I dare you to get immersed in your life's mission, whatever it may be. There's no half-stepping. When you move tenaciously in the direction of your vision, your vision moves tenaci-ously toward you. "No man can stop the man with a plan because no one has a plan to stop him" (unknown).

How long will you keep on keeping on? It would have been so easy for one young man to bow his head in shame and give up. He failed in business in 1831, he was defeated for the legislature in '32, he was elected to the legislature in '34, his sweetheart died in '35, he had a nervous breakdown in '36, he was defeated for Speaker in '38, he was defeated for elector in '40, he was defeated for Congress in '43, he was elected to Congress in '48, he was defeated for the Senate in '50, and he was defeated for Vice President in '56 and for the Senate in '58. But in 1860, he was elected President of the United States. His name was Abraham Lincoln.[3]

Sir Winston Churchill learned a lot about persever-ance. He said, "Success is going from failure to failure without loss of enthusiasm."[4] A few days after his election as Britain's Prime Minister in 1940, the 65-year-old delivered his famous "blood, toil, tears and sweat" address:

Victory is our aim, victory at all costs, victory in spite of terror, victory, however long and hard the road may be; for without victory there is no survival.[5] He also said: *There comes a special moment in everyone's life, a moment for which that person was born. That special opportunity, when he seizes it, will fulfill his mission — a mission for which he is uniquely qualified. In that moment he finds greatness.*[6]

Churchill led with courage and strong determination. "His bull-dog determination smashed through every obstacle that stood in the road of victory. Dubbed the "bulldog warrior," Friend and foe alike knew the meaning of his raised two forefingers which formed a "V" –victory at all costs.[7] When passion blends with purpose, an unbeatable force emerges. Like a tidal wave, it lifts the possessor toward what some would call unattainable heights.

On a Thursday evening in December 1955, after a long day of work as a seamstress for a Montgomery, Alabama, department store, a woman named Rosa Parks boarded a city bus en route to her home.

She walked past the first few mostly empty rows of seats marked "Whites Only." It was against the law for an African American to sit in those seats, so she occupied a seat in the middle of the bus.

After several stops, the bus maxed out. The driver noticed that all the seats in the "Whites Only" section were taken, and that more white passengers had just boarded. He ordered the people in Mrs. Parks' row to move to the back of the bus, where there were no open seats. At first, no one budged. But then the driver barked at the black passengers a second time and they all got up, except for Rosa Parks. [9]

Subsequently, the Sheriff was called in and Rosa Parks was arrested and sent to jail. Her act of passion

led to the eruption of the already simmering Civil Rights Movement with Martin Luther King Jr. at the helm — a movement that has given previously denied rights to blacks and other minorities.

GETTING BACK ON OFFENSE

The life of Helen Keller, an inspirational author and activist who was both blind and deaf, takes away the defense of those who use petty excuses for failure to rise in the world. She wrote, "Character cannot be developed in ease and quiet. Only through experience of trial and suffering can the soul be strengthened, vision cleared, ambition inspired and success achie-ved."[9]

When I embarked upon my writing career, there was no time to learn the keys on the keyboard; a high school dropout, I had never taken a typing class. But I wanted to write. It was as if a dam of inspiration had burst open. So, my right hand did the talking while the keyboard did the walking. Today, several scripts and a book later, I still type with my right hand. Some people wait for the right moment to do things. For them, everything has to be perfect before seizing the opportunity. But great achievers have an abundance of "iron in their blood" and accomplish worthwhile feats, obstacles or no obstacles. Author Dr. Sidney N. Bremer says in his book *Spirit of Apollo*, "No matter what your position in life may be or the conditions which hem you in, there will be a tide in your affairs which, taken at its flood leads on to fortune. But you must be ready to take that chance."[10]

So many people allow handicaps to keep them from achieving victory. A man of character sees a victory in every adversity. There could have been hundreds of people with the potential of Abraham Lincoln, Rosa Parks, Martin Luther King Jr., Winston Churchill and Helen Keller born during their time. But because those hundreds resisted change, their contribution to mankind remains undefined.

Change is tough because it takes you out of your comfort zone. It stretches you and puts you face to face with the unknown. In the Bible, Jacob's real change occurred after he wrestled with God. Once you embrace change, the Creator will provide the supernatural resources necessary to impact your life. He will build a bridge across the gulf of impossibility, but it's up to you to accept the adventure and cross that bridge. There's no more impressive sight in society than that of a young man fired up with passion and purpose. He's bound to win; the world stands aside to let him pass.

DREAM BIGGER

How big is your dream? Is it a cause greater than yourself? You will not make it upstream with only a mere wish. The rapids are fierce; they'll push you back downstream toward self pity and mediocrity if your resolve isn't strong enough.

NINE KEY POINTS TO REALIZING YOUR DREAM

1. Focus on a big dream that includes others; By empowering others you will in turn become empowered.
2. Start with whatever is in your heart right now, and trust your hunch — that invisible voice that breathes life into your vision. Someday your acorn of desire may become a full- grown oak.

3. Increase your self worth by trusting in the power greater than yourself. Put God in the drivers' seat.

4. Become passionate about your vision. Aim high, work hard, and think creatively, and the dream that others call impossible will be yours for the taking. They will eventually applaud you as you cross the finish line.

5. Tenaciously pursue your dream in the face of setbacks, even failures. Stay focused. Failure itself is never the tragedy; low aim is the tragedy.

6. Watch out for dream stealers. They come in the form of family and well-meaning friends. Just about anybody will say no to your idea, and you'll have numerous reasons for quitting along the way. It's always the finish — not the start — that counts.

7. Do something daily to nurture and support your dream. Remember, the dream isn't worth having unless you enjoy the journey.

8. Prepare yourself mentally. As Louis Pasteur said, "Chance favors only the prepared mind."[11]

9. Be persistent. A huge tree doesn't tumble with one swing of the axe. You've got to keep swinging. If you can dream it, you can have it.

VISION IS THE KEY

Your aim needs to be as bold as your courage, not as timid as your fear. German poet Johann Wolfgang von Goethe said this:"Whatever you can do, or dream you can do, begin it. Boldness has genius, power, and magic in it."[12] Author James Allen stated, "Columbus cherished a vision of another world and he discovered it;

Copernicus fostered a vision of a multiplicity of worlds and a wider universe, and he revealed it."[13] Martin Luther King Jr. dreamed of an America where black kids and white kids would hold hands and walk together and it has come to pass. Humanity, though sometimes anti-visionary, never forgets its dreamers.

The man who has triumphed over difficulty — who has a vision and achieves it — bears signs of victory on his face. He seems to glow with triumph in every movement. The winner's circle embraces him.

I've been a church member at Oasis Christian Center in Los Angeles for almost five years now. My life has changed for the better, in part because of the influ-ence of senior pastors Philip and Holly Wagner. They started with a few members a little over 20 years ago and now lead a 2,000 strong growing congregation. In an effort to accommodate the growth, they recently moved to a much larger facility, which maxed out for both services on Easter Sunday. Their focus is on touching the world, and they have caught onto a great challenge of service with magnificent obsession. The church is seeing victory after victory, and their mission outreach programs will no doubt have a lasting effect on the world.

DEVELOP A MAGNETIC PERSONALITY

What you love and how you love defines who you are. Have you ever seen someone enter a room and immediately — charismatically — attract the warmth and attention of others? Some personalities are like that. Whether you meet them on top of a mountain or down in a valley. In good times and in bad, they have a way of attracting people.

These twelve things can be said about such a person:

- He has conquered selfishness; others have become his priority.

- He knows that he will reap what he sows.

- He exercises self control.
- He listens to others.

- He gives with no strings attached.

- He recognizes the value in others.

- He appreciates what others intend, not only what they do.

- He lifts others up.

- He's positive.

- He leads and inspires others.

- He possesses a servant's heart.

- He keeps increasing his own value.

John 3:16 is one of the most profound passages of scripture. It tells us this: "God so loved the world that he gave his one and only Son so that whosoever believeth in him may not be lost, but have everlasting life." This verse represents love unabridged. It shows that God is love. He delights in coming through for you just as He did for the three Hebrew boys in the fiery furnace, Daniel in the lions' den and the children of Israel crossing the Red Sea. In love, He offers you eternal life through His Son, Jesus Christ.

How do you love others? James 2:8 says, "This royal law is found in the scriptures: 'Love your neighbor as you love yourself.' If you obey this law, you are doing right." Jesus painted this picture in the story of The Good Samaritan, who stepped up when the religious people of his day overlooked a man who was robbed, beaten and left by the side of the road (Luke 10:25-37).

"From everyone who has been given much, much will be demanded." Luke 12:48 says. There's something special about a child of God who has gone through tough times and gotten back up. Have you ever been in the sphere of such an individual and felt totally blessed? It's inescapable! That person has developed a strong relationship with God out of a need to seek and find Him regularly. He has created such a bond with God that the overspill has become contagious, setting off a brush fire of love in your heart. You want to be around that kind of person.

After a decade-long fight with leukemia, the teenage daughter of one of our pastors and my great friend, Gary Kooper, went home to be with the Lord. At the memorial service in her honor, I watched as tremen-dous amounts of love poured out from the congre-gation, mainly from couples who had been coached by Gary and his wife, and some whom he had joined in holy matrimony.

A few weeks later I had lunch with him. As we broke bread together, verses of scripture poured from him like a flowing stream. I united pen and paper, trying not to miss a thing. Not once did he talk about his loss. But what he had gained was worth my docu-menting: an abundance of God's rich promises. When we parted that afternoon, I left spiritually filled. He's a man of stalwart character, and I'm proud to call him a friend.

DEVELOP FRIENDSHIPS

When you want to convert a man to your view, you go over to where he's standing, take him by the hand and guide him; you don't call him a dummy; you don't order him to come over where you are. You start where he is, and work from that position. That's the only way to get him to budge.[14] — Thomas Aquinas

To paraphrase Mr. Philip Wagner from his "iLove" message:

- Accept people and embrace their differences. Throw out the mindset of "If you pass my battery of tests, then I'll love you." Remember: To love is natural, but to love unconditionally is supernatural.

- Demonstrate acts of kindness. Give legs to the love you have for someone by showing it in practical ways, as God has for us. Remember: People don't care what you know until they know how much you care.

- Make a connection. It's possible to work, hang out and even live with someone without making a meaningful connection. Connecting requires openness, honesty and sharing of your life. Remember: People love to talk about themselves.

- Be loyal. Earn the trust of others, and don't take for granted the most trustworthy people in your life. Express love and appreciation for them more than anyone else. Remember: Loyal friends are hard to find and harder to keep.[15]

Love should be like a never-ending stream. The more you pour out, the more you find to pour.

MOM'S UNDYING LOVE

As a kid I had the opportunity of seeing love in action seven out of seven. My mom, though a victim of poor academicals, wasted not a single moment working endlessly and tirelessly by day, and nightly encour-aging us around a kerosene lamp – back then we didn't have electricity. She wanted all nine us to be endowed in our chosen calling; opportunities which she never had. With smoke in our eyes we burned the midnight oil in our effort to excel. When Dad passed on in 1967, a financial reverse begun, mom fought through it and with some of her meager resources saw me through most of high school. I remembered her saying "John, this is all I can afford."

Despite not having riches and only just enough, along with a busy lifestyle, she found time to open her door to a stranger, neighbor or friend – providing them with a warm meal while she articulated about God's unfailing love. She cared for the sick, and the needy, shared groceries with them and most of all commu-nicated her faith in God. I witnessed many lives changed; because she cared. Although we didn't have all the gadgets as other kids did back then, she taught us how to share whatever little we had.

Mom's multiple battles with Alzheimer's disease for almost two decades ended in 2005. However, her undying love lives on today and will for many generations.

LEAD BY EXAMPLE

Leadership is all about character. A true leader inspires followers, and in order to develop leaders, you must become a better leader yourself. That comes by changing and growing.

In his book *Life is Tremendous,* Charlie Jones states, "Everyone is responsible for something he alone must do. If we enjoy the privilege and discharge our obligation, we grow; if we ignore our opportunity, we join the shrinking violets of humanity. The most tremendous experience of life is the learning process. The saddest time is when a person thinks that he has learned enough."[16] God has given each of us talents and abilities just as he did in the story of the ten talents (Matt. 25:14-30). What we do with what we've been given determines who we are. We either *use* it or *lose* it.

Great leaders use what's been given to them and are not afraid to fail. They're cut from the fabric of persistency. Education is not always a requirement for such a calling, and most begin with genuine handicaps.

Nothing in the world can take the place of persistence. Talent will not. Nothing is more common than unsuccess-ful men with talent. Genius will not. Unrewarded genius is almost a proverb. Education will not. The world is full of educated derelicts. Persistence, determination and hard work make the difference.[17] — Calvin Coolidge

In order to lead, you must have someone following you. And in order to have a following, you must develop trust. Trust lies at the core of strong character formation. "No man can climb out beyond the limi-tations of his own character,"[18] John Morley said. Just as the "things which proceed out of the mouth come from the heart and they defile the man" (Matt. 15:18 KJV), lack of trustworthiness in a person shows weak character.

BECOME A WINNER

Losers let things happen, but winners make things happen. Winners are never satisfied with who they are, and therefore, they're constantly working on changing and enhancing their self-image. They have a vision of the person they want to become, and they develop a well-defined, emotional picture of them-selves as if they have already achieved that goal. Advance-winning pumps through their veins.

- They breathe the championship.

- They feel drenched from the entire bucket of Gatorade poured over their head.

- They experience the thrill of Disneyland before playing the Super Bowl.

- They caress the Oscar.

- They hear the crowd's approval.

- They feel the gold medal around their neck.
- They see a church with one million members worshipping in spirit and truth.

- They stand tall in the winner's circle.

- They feel their new self-image in advance.

- They dress rehearse receiving the Nobel Prize.

Winners let nothing stand in the way of victory. You can smell their tenacity like expensive cologne beca-use they have a feeling of their own worth. They think, "I can, I will, and I shall not be denied."

The power of your purpose depends wholly on the vigor and determination behind it.

To paraphrase Dr. Bremer: Your resolute will and firm determination to succeed will carry you up-stream, no matter how strong the current or how tough the obstacles in your way. But if your will is fragile and your determination wavering, you will float downstream with the multitudes of others who, like a dead fish, have not enough zest or willpower to force their way upstream.[19]

A reservoir of water will not quench a city's thirst, nor put out fires, if it is not allowed to circulate in the mains and service pipes.

— Sidney N. Bremer

5

CHANGE YOUR WORLD

Dr. Bremer wrote, "The world wants your best, and you should resolve early in life never to give anything but the best of which you are capable."[1]

What is your purpose here on earth? Few people know why they're here and what their destiny is, so they place very little value on their life and the lives of others. It's amazing, though, to see the transfor-mation that takes place as soon as a person discovers his true purpose in life — and takes up the challenge. Some people search all their lives and never find it, and others find it and refuse to accept it because they feel unworthy.

Moses, for one, felt inadequate when God called him to lead the children of Israel out of slavery. "But Moses said to God, 'I am not a great man! How can I go to the King and lead the Israelites out of Egypt?'" (Exod. 3:11) And yet, through eventual — although reluctant — willingness to accept God's call, with the aid of his brother, Aaron, Moses experienced a life filled with mountain top experiences and miracles:

- His rod turned into a serpent in Pharaoh's presence (Exod. 7:10).

- Water turned into blood (Exod. 7:20).

- Frogs covered the land of Egypt (Exod. 8:5).

- The Lord struck down every Egyptian firstborn (Exod. 12:29).

- God parted the Red Sea (Exod. 14:21).

- Manna fell from the sky (Exod. 16:15).

- Moses received the Ten Commandments, written with the finger of God, on Mt. Sinai (Exod. 31:18).

Moses' life changed from "Who am I?" to the recip-ient of the Ten Commandments from God's own hand.

In Genesis 28:12, Jacob, who had stolen his brother's birthright, dreamed he saw a ladder set upon the earth, the top of it reaching to heaven, with angels of God ascending and descending on it. "And behold the Lord stood above it, and said, 'I am the Lord God of Abraham thy father, and the God of Isaac: the land whereon thou liest, to thee will I give it, and to thy seed'." (Gen. 28:13 KJV) Jacob's changed life after he was forgivingly blessed by his father Isaac (Gen. 28: 1) was rewarded with family and estate blessings. He also received a name change to "Israel" synonymous with blessings, after wrestling with God, (Gen. 32:22-32). Later when he came face to face with his brother Esau from whom he fled after forging the acceptance of his birthright, Jacob forgivingly sought to please Esau and even addressed him as *master*. Gen. 33:10-11 says: "Jacob said, 'No! Please! If I have pleased you, then accept the gift I give you. I'm happy to see your face again. It is like seeing the face of God, because you have accepted me. So I beg you to accept the gift I give you. God has been very good to me, and I have more than I need.' And because Jacob begged. Esau accepted the gift." What a change in the lives of both men!

At the top of this staircase your transformation awaits you: A beautiful enhanced life; others will seek you out in order to remold their lives and character. Will you trade your heart of stone for one of moldable clay and allow the Master Potter to work on you? If so, you're almost ready for the transformation you deserve. You will set the world on fire with your illumination. It will be all about what people see in you — not something you have to push on them or try to prove.

This final step — changing your world — is your freedom ticket. You're about to discover the new you as you move forward with your life. But first, you must surrender your life to the Potter. And you also need to remove any emotional scars that alienate you from the life you're entitled to live.

If you have been hurt by someone in the past, you probably try to guard against future injury. In doing so, you form a "spiritual callus," which is like an emotional scar, to protect your ego. And that creates an emotional wall that no one has the ability to scale. A church member who has been the subject of wrongful criticism by a church leader may choose to never again attend that church or another house of worship.

In his book on *Psycho-Cybernetics*, Dr. Maxwell Maltz discusses removing the emotional scars in your life. To paraphrase Dr. Maltz:

- A child who has had his ego sliced up by a repressive and cruel parent or teacher vows   to never trust another authority figure.

- A man whose love has been rejected by a woman vows to never again become romantically involved.

- A woman who has been hurt by one man vows to never trust another man again.[2]

Dr. Maltz continues, "As in the case of a facial scar, excessive protection against the original source of injury can make us more vulnerable, and do us more damage in other areas. The person who feels 'lonely' or out of touch with other human beings, also feels out of touch with his real self and with life."[3] The emotional wall you build as a protection against one person can cut you off from other human beings and even from yourself.

Emotional scars can create juvenile delinquents. Psychiatrist Bernard Holland said "that although juvenile delinquents appear to be independent and are known to brag — particularly about how they hate everyone in authority — they protest too much. Underneath this hard exterior, he says, "is a soft inner person who wants to depend on others."[4] However, they seem to not want to get close to anyone. They will not trust others and always seem to have their defense antennas up.

Emotional scars to our ego have another adverse effect. As Dr. Maltz explained, "They tend to lead to the development of a scarred, marred self-image; the picture of a person not liked or accepted by other human beings, the picture of a person who can't get along well in the world in which he lives."[5]

Emotional scars prevent you from changing your life. They prevent you from becoming what professor of educational psychology Dr. Arthur W. Combs called a "self-fulfilled person."[6] This should be your ulti-mate goal, he said, but it's not something with which you're born; it must be achieved. Jacob removed the emotional scar of stealing his brother's birthright by seeking forgiveness and was immensely blessed.

According to Dr. Maltz, self-fulfilled people have the following characteristics:[7]

- They see themselves as liked, wanted, acceptable and able individuals.

- They have a high degree of acceptance for who they are.

- They have a feeling of oneness with others.

- They have a rich store of information and knowledge.

"The person with emotional scars not only has a self-image of an unwanted, unliked and incapable person, but he also has an image of the world in which he lives as a hostile place," Maltz adds.[8]

How do you change your self-image? By changing the way you are.

Before I rededicated my life to the Lord almost five years ago, I struggled with my setbacks in life and felt animosity toward everyone who had wronged me and wanted to see my family fall apart. However, it was not until I put everyone's name on a list and prayed individually for their forgiveness and mine that I received true freedom from my emotional imprisonment. Today, my life is one of fullness and trust because I've allowed change to permeate my entire being.

A car's rearview mirror is smaller than its windshield for a reason. Yet most people spend their lives look-ing through their rearview mirror. Unconditional forgiveness will release you from the vice of your enemies and set you up for success. Your changed life is beckoning.

God wants to bless you. He's standing at the door to usher you in. "Come unto me, all ye that labour and are heavy laden, and I will give you rest." (Matt. 11:28) By surrendering your will to Him, you are automatically placing Him in the driver's seat of your life. And He knows every pothole, intersection and traffic signal.

The world has been searching for you. It needs people who will step up and stand in the gap — those who aren't afraid to step off the sidelines and into the game. You've acquired knowledge and wisdom among these pages, and the past can no longer hold you in its cocoon. By changing who you are, you've equipped yourself to change your world. The five steps to changing your life help you breathe victory daily. You may not be a Winston Churchill, Martin Luther King Jr., Abraham Lincoln, Helen Keller, Rosa Parks, Mother Teresa,

Columbus, Moses or Jacob. But you are YOU — right here, right now. Will you of strong character embrace the world? What could *you* do with the determination of some of the afore-mentioned personalities? Will this world become a better place because *you* embraced change?

My hope is that, by now, you've found a cause greater than yourself and are ready to take charge of your destiny. Dr. King said: "If a man hasn't discov-ered something that he will die for, he isn't fit to live."[9] YOU are chosen, and the world needs you.

NOTES

~

Introduction

1. UBR, Inc., The American, The New Business Magazine For People Who Think.
http://www.people.ubr.com/

2. James Allen, *As a Man Thinketh* (New York: Bantam Books Inc., 1982), 111.

Prelude to Chapter 1:

Allen, *As a Man Thinketh*, 110.

Chapter 1: Change Your Thoughts

1. Allen, *As a Man Thinketh*, 107.

2. Francis P. Martin, *Hung by the Tongue*, (Lafayette, LA: Francis P. Martin Bible Teaching Seminars, Books and Tapes, 1987), 18.

3. Napoleon Hill, *Think and Grow Rich* (Chatsworth: Wilshire Book Company, 1999), 12.

4. Ibid., 16 and 320.

5. BrainyQuote, "JFK Quotes" www.brainyquote.com/quotes/quotes/j/johnfkenn132742.html

6. David Schwartz, *The Magic of Thinking Big*, First Fireside Edition (New York: Simon & Schuster, Inc., 1987), 188.

7. Claude Bristol, *The Magic of Believing* (Englewood Cliffs, N.J.: Prentice Hall, Inc., 1957), 22.

8. BrainyQuote, "Victor Hugo Quotes," http://www.brainyquote.com/authors/v/victor_hugo.html.

9. Warren Bennis, *On Becoming a Leader*, Ontario & New York
10. Addison-Wesley Publishing Company, Inc., 1990), 143.

11. Bristol, *The Magic of Believing*, 21.

12. Hill, *Think and Grow Rich*, 126.

13. BrainyQuote, "Pascal Quotes," http://www.brainyquote.com/quotes/quotes/b/blaisepasc133798.html

14. Skip Ross with Carole C. Carlson, *Say Yes to Your Potential* (Rockford, MI: Circle "A" Productions, 1983), 13.

Chapter 2: Change Your Words

1. David Swartz, Magic of Self-Direction, Cornerstone Library, Simon & Schuster, New York, 1982), 12.

2. Martin, *Hung by the Tongue*, 9.

3. Kendall White, Critical Issue, Youth Motivation, NASE http://www.self-esteem-nase.org/kendallwhite.shtml.

4. Dale Sabin, Divorce Stats. http://www.modestapparelchristianclothinglydia ofpurpledressecustomsewing.com/divorce_stats.h tm.

5. T. D. Jakes messages: *Chosen, Seven Steps To a Turnaround, Dreams.* The Potters House, Dallas, Texas,

Prelude to Chapter 3:

William Danforth, *I Dare You* (St. Louis: American Youth Foundation, 1991), 13.

Chapter 3: Change Your Actions

1. Keith DeGreen, *Creating a Success Environment* (New York: New Bantam Books Inc., 1982), 62.

2. Danforth, *I Dare You*, 8.

3. Ibid., 5.

4. Ibid., 14.

5. Les Brown, *Live Your Dreams* (New York: William Morrow & Company, Inc., 1992), 86.

6. Schwartz, *The Magic of Thinking Big*, 22.

7. Danforth, *I Dare You*, 11.

8. Ibid., 10.

Prelude to Chapter 4:

John C. Maxwell, *Talent is Never Enough,* Nashville, Thomas Nelson, Inc., 2007), 28.

Chapter 4: Change Your Character

1. Adele Q. Brown, Martin Luther King Jr., World Alamanac Milwaukee, Library, (Gareth Stevens Inc. 2004), 31.

2. Norman Vincent Peale, *You Can If You Think You Can* (New York: Prentice Hall Press) 1986, 15.

3. Alan Loy McGinnis, *Bringing Out the Best in People* (Minneapolis: Augsburg Publishing House, 1985), 76.

4. Philip Baker, *Secret of Super Achievers* (New Kensington: Whitaker House, 2005), 77.

5. Sidney N. Bremer, *Spirit of Apollo,* Lexington, Kentucky, Successful Achievement Inc. 1971), 101.

6. Live My Passion, http://www.livemypassion.com/thoughts.htm.

7. Bremer, *Spirit of Apollo,* 101.

8. Sitting Down, 2007-1996 Scholastic Inc, http://teacher.scholastic.com/rosa/sittingdown.htm.

9. Baker, *Secret of Super Achievers*, 74.

10. Bremer, *Spirit of Apollo,* 134.

11. BrainyQuote, "Louis Pasteur Quotes," http://www.brainyquote.com/quotes/authors/l/louis_paster. html.

12. BrainyQuote, Johann Wolfgang von Goethe Quotes," http://www.brainyquote.com/quotes/authors/j/johann_wolfgang_von_goeth.html.

13. Allen, *As a Man Thinketh*, 110.

14. McGinnis, *Bringing Out the Best*, 141.

15. Philip Wagner, *iLove Message*, iSeries, Oasis Christian Center, Los Angeles, California, 2007.

16. Charlie "Tremendous" Jones, *Life is Tremendous* (Wheaton: Tyndale House Publishers, Inc., 1968), 9.

17. Ross, *Say Yes to Your Potential*, 145-146.

18. BrainyQuote, John Morley Quotes," http://www.whatquote.com/quotes/John-Morley/23160-No-man-can-climb-out.htm.

19. Bremer, Spirit of Apollo, 103.

Prelude to Chapter 5:

Bremer, *Spirit of Apollo*, 300.

Chapter 5: Change Your World

1. Bremer, *Spirit of Apollo*, 155.

2. Maxwell Maltz, M.D., *Psycho-Cybernetics* (Englewood Cliffs, N.J.: Pocket Books Inc., 1960), 151.

3. Ibid., 152.

4. Ibid., 152-153

5. Ibid., 152.

6. Ibid., 153.

7. Ibid., 153.

8. Ibid., 153.

9. Life of Dr. King,
   www.webstar.co.uk/~ubugaje/**luther**3.html.

Unless otherwise indicated in the text, all Bible references used are from the New Century Version: Word Publishing, Thomas Nelson Inc., Belgium, 1991),

About The AUTHOR

John A. Andrews was born in the Islands of St. Vincent and the Grenadines. He grew up in a home of five sisters and three brothers. His parents were all about values: work hard, love God and never give up on dreams.

As a self-educated student John developed an interest for music. Although lacking the formal education he later put his knowledge and passion to good use, moonlighting as a disc jockey in New York. This paved the way for further exploration in the entertainment world. John's acting career began 12 years ago. Leaving the Big Apple for Los Angeles a decade ago, not only put several national TV commercials under his belt but helped him to find his niche.

He read his first positive thinking book *"The Magic of Thinking Big"* 23 years ago and consequently developed an insatiable appetite for inspirational material.

John states: "Some people create, while others compete. Creating is where the rubber meets the road. A dream worth having is one worth fighting for because freedom is not free; it carries a massive price tag."

*   *   *

What makes these men tick? What causes them to rise to the occasion no matter what comes against them? Is it something they were born with - inherited from their genes? Is it some-thing they acquire from the leaders who, as if by design, step into their life? Is it the refining process which brings out the best in them during their struggle to swim upstream?

Come with me as I take you on my 10 year will-not-be-denied journey through "venomous" Hollywood, the hub of the entertainment industry, where the stakes are high, dreamers as well as dream-killers are plentiful, where hard work, guts and determination is the call, or if by mere luck nepotism finds you. So many claim to have a dream, yet they give up when attacked by the snakelike attitude of the dream crushers of today. They lose their will to persist, failing to stand when the dust settles.

Fasten your seatbelt!

SPREAD SOME LOVE (RELATIONSHIPS 101)

WORKBOOK

Three weeks after the release of the foundation to this workbook "Spread Some Love (Relationships 101)," I was doing a book signing event at a restaurant in Southern California. A woman came up to me and asked if she can scan through my new volume. I enthusiastically gave her the go ahead. Before wrapping the event some two hours later, I noticed that she was not only still holding the book in her hands but was joined by four other women - all in their late 20's to early 30's. I stepped into their space and after introducing myself, joined their huddle. I asked where everyone was in their relationships with a significant other. I learned that two of them were married, two were still single and one was going through a divorce – they weren't very passionate about their relational status.

The woman going through her divorce asked me what motivated me to write such a book. I responded enthusiastically: "Doctors go to school for a reason, so do lawyers, pastors keep studying in order to remain on the pulpit but we fail to work on our relationships on a daily basis. Many of us fall in love and expect that osmosis will pull every-thing together. It doesn't - It can't." She sobbingly echoed: "where were you a year ago." That hit home. A year too late I pondered - her marriage would have been saved. **Writing this workbook was inescapable!**

SPREAD SOME LOVE (Relationships 101)

SPREAD SOME LOVE (Relationships 101) was born out of his failed marriage which ended after 13 years in 2000. Since then John has not only read dozens of books on relationships but has associated with several experts on this subject, including Pastors Philip and Holly Wagner, whose marriage is now entering its 24th year. As an entrepreneur and sought after coach, Mr. Andrews believes that marriages should last forever and states: "If a person isn't willing to work on him or herself they should stay out of the falling in love business; the world is full of too many abandoned relationships and broken hearts."

MOVIE BASED ON THE BOOK:

SPREAD SOME LOVE (RELATIONSHIPS 101)

DOCU-DRAMA

This 60 minute slice of life Docu-drama comes filled with beats cemented in relational mystique. This DVD features elite relationship interviews, dramatic scenes, unique historical footage, sizzling music and much more.

A Jon Jef Jam Entertainment

&

Johaandrews.com 2009 Production

UPSTREAM SWIMMING

AUDIO CD

CONTACT INFORMATION

For more information about *JOHN A. ANDREWS*, to book speaking engagements, sign up for his mailings, purchase his books and learn more about BOOKS THAT WILL ENHANCE YOUR LIFE ™, visit his website at:

www. JOHNAANDREWS.COM

or

Contact John at:

BOOKS THAT WILL ENHANCE YOUR LIFE™
P.O. BOX 56298
SHERMAN OAKS,
CA 91413

CPSIA information can be obtained at www.ICGtesting.com
Printed in the USA
BVOW051804051011

272926BV00001B/33/P